OUT OF THE DUST

BY ANNE FRANCIS

Published to commemorate the 50th Anniversary
of St. George's Crypt, Leeds

ST GEORGES CRYPT

“Who is like the Lord our God, who is seated on high, who looks far down upon the heavens and the earth? He raises the poor from the dust, and lifts the needy from the ash heap, to make them sit with princes, with the princes of His people.”

Psalm 113:5-8 R.S.V.

FOREWORDS

From the former Bishop of Knaresborough

As one who worked with Don Robins from the early days of the Crypt as a layman, a theological student and a curate I am deeply thankful that under the good hand of God the work which Don started has developed in such a remarkable way.

I thank God that the Crypt has now reached its 50th birthday and I pray that God will bless all who work there and all who use the services it offers in the future.

I have pleasure in commending this book which gives an account of the expanding work and brings up to date the story of the Crypt.

Ralph Emmerson

From the Assistant Chief Constable
West Yorkshire Metropolitan Police

It is with considerable pleasure that I have accepted the opportunity to contribute to the foreword of this book, but you may wonder why this should be provided by a member of the Police Service. The reason is that the Police Service is also a caring service. In addition to the police officer's responsibility for law and order and the preservation of peace, he or she also has a responsibility for the community — and that must include all its members. Because of their availability at all hours, whether on the streets of the city or at Police Stations, police officers have to be involved in the general problems of the community. The police know that for men in need of shelter for the night, or some form of care, St. George's Crypt fills a void that is not filled by the State. This applies in particular to men who otherwise would more than likely be sleeping in derelict premises or in the open and who, as a result, might fall victim to worse situations or find themselves in conflict with the law.

The police are particularly aware of the necessary work undertaken by the Crypt today. Over the years willing helpers have shared in this work, expressing their concern for others in feeding, clothing and providing medical care for those in need of such help.

I end by paying tribute, on behalf of the Police Service in Leeds, to the work of the Crypt and reminding all of the need for such a service. This refuge within a church must symbolise something of what fellowship and charity should mean in a Christian society.

S. Boothroyd

CONTENTS

CHAPTER		*PAGE*
1	THE OLD CROW	1
2	THEIR FATHER'S HOUSE	8
3	A NEW ERA	15
4	DAY BY DAY	23
5	THE STATE TAKES CARE OF ALL THAT . . . DOESN'T IT?	31
6	DUST TO DUST	37
7	RICH IN FAITH	43
8	A PLACE TO CALL HOME	51
9	DOCTOR IN THE HOUSE	59
10	AN INFINITE CAPACITY FOR BEING LET DOWN	66
11	LOAVES AND FISHES	70
12	SOMETHING MORE — a personal postscript	74

Many people have contributed to the production of this book, whether by sharing memories or experiences of the work of the Crypt, by taking photographs, by offering editorial advice, or by typing manuscripts. I would like to thank all who have participated in any way.

CHAPTER 1

THE OLD CROW

"Where are you going with a shovel and a barrow?" challenged Horace Stacey, church verger. He was addressing a slight, wiry man in his late forties. "I got my meals at the Crypt," came the reply, "and I think it only fair that I should pay for it in kind."

It was a February morning in 1962 and Bryan[1] was helping to clear the church of rubble from the spire, which had partially collapsed in severe gales during the night. This was the first encounter between the two men, but it marked the beginning of a deep and lasting friendship.

It had been two years earlier that Bryan first appeared at the Crypt. Following his discharge from the Army after 30 years (all his adult life) he found the freedom of civilian life bewildering. It was difficult to find employment, and he had begun to drink heavily to overcome his disillusionment. Eventually he found a job in a pottery, but by now his mental state was unsettled. He grew obsessed with what seemed to him the injustice of taxation and one day resolved never to work again if it meant paying tax.

Among the men who came to the Crypt, Bryan

1 This is his real name. Except for staff, all other names in this book are fictitious, although the events are all true.

stood out because of his smart appearance and passion for cleanliness. He was most fastidious about polishing his boots daily (Army fashion) and would wear his two shirts and two pairs of socks on alternate days, washing the soiled garments and hanging them on the church railings to dry!

When it was suggested that he might like to help in the kitchen he tackled the job with characteristic thoroughness, revealing a great talent for getting a job done before anyone else had even noticed it needed doing. He voluntarily took on more and more and before long was responsible for opening the gate in the morning and locking up at night.

Bryan found his work at the Crypt satisfying, but the drink problem was ever present. He would go regularly across the road to his local "The George", sometimes returning in aggressive mood and causing trouble with the men. This gave the Crypt workers a few headaches as Bryan was regarded by the rest of the men as "staff". He did not sleep at the Crypt but made himself a niche in the coal-hole of the school next to the church, and this was his home for many years.

The first time Horace asked Bryan if he would come into church the retort was "Not -------- likely!" But the following week, the invitation repeated, came a grudging and abrupt, "I'll come and have a look." Once this first barrier was broken, Bryan was eager to help Horace in his duties as verger. He stopped drinking on Saturday nights in order to be fit for work on Sunday mornings.

One Sunday Horace was preparing the communion table while Bryan was checking the pews. "Give me a hand a minute, Bryan. I've got this cloth twisted." "I'm not coming through there," asserted Bryan, and marched out of the church muttering, leaving Horace with his hands full and the cloth in a tangle. Bryan returned. "What did you say you wanted?" "Just help me get this cloth untwisted," repeated Horace. "I'm not coming through them rails!" — again Bryan marched off down the church and again he came back. This time, overcoming his fear of the sanctuary he went to Horace's aid. He drew the line at touching the cloth with his hands, however, and somehow managed to sort out the muddle using his elbows!

Bryan felt he had no right to approach God, whom he saw as very high up and remote, inaccessible to anyone except the clergy. He was very conscious of his own lowly state after the authority and prestige he had known as a Regimental Sergeant Major in his Army days and believed that the Crypt, and not the church, was where he belonged. But he was searching, and from time to time Horace shared something of the Gospel with him. He often referred to the story of Peter, who had enjoyed the honour of being one of the Lord's closest followers and yet sank to the level where he denied his Master.

Horace was, of course, by no means the only one seeking to make Jesus real to Bryan. George Goldsack, Crypt Secretary for many years and Don Paterson, the Warden, also ministered to him, and many others were praying for him.

Gradually Bryan changed. His righteous wrath descended upon any one he heard taking the Lord's name in vain, although formerly he had been among the chief offenders. He had never been an easy-going man and still loved an argument, but could not bear to be on unfriendly terms with anyone for more than the briefest interlude. He used to go to any lengths to make his peace without actually having to apologise but now he was learning how to say "I'm sorry". He was unstintingly generous and loved children, who were also instinctively drawn to him. No doubt he was attracted by their simplicity and sincerity — they neither probed nor preached but accepted him just as he was.

He still found any stress outside of normal routine difficult to cope with and when things got on top of him he would disappear, sometimes for days, sometimes weeks. Once he disappeared for four months. One of the Crypt workers was getting married and invited Bryan to the wedding. Bryan prepared the church and saw that everything was ready, but the night before the wedding he vanished. Months later, as Horace was unlocking the school gates one morning, Bryan emerged from the coal-hole. The approaching schoolchildren saw him and the excited cry went up, "It's Bryan!" Bryan had come home.

Towards the end of the 1960s Bryan became ill and had tests and treatment at Leeds General Infirmary. In 1974 he became ill again and underwent an operation for cancer of the bladder. The Vicar visited him in hospital and was intrigued when Bryan insisted on leading him along a corridor and into the toilets. "If I look through this window," said Bryan with great satisfaction, "I can just see St. George's and the Crypt." He was moved by the fact that members of the church and Crypt staff visited him in hospital and began to think more deeply about the Gospel. After this illness he never touched alcohol again and devoted himself entirely to his work in the Crypt and the church. He started to listen to Christian talks and songs on a tape recorder and even to attend Sunday services.

It had taken a long, long time, but through the continuing love and concern of people such as Horace, George, Don and others, Bryan had at last come to recognize that God loved him. Horace, anxious to be sure of Bryan's position, asked him one day, "Have you put your hand in the hand of the One who loves you?" "Yes", replied Bryan. "Have you really?" "I said yes didn't I?" "And you're quite definite about it?" pressed Horace. "If I said yes then I meant yes," rejoined Bryan, annoyed, "what have you got to ask me three times for?" "You are not the only one to be asked three times," replied Horace, reminding Bryan once again of the story of Peter, which they had talked about so often.

Bryan was officially made Assistant Verger and the long black gown he now wore soon earned him the nickname of "The Old Crow". He was provided with a room on the church premises which he arranged in spotless precision with his medals in pride of place above his bed. Before long a label appeared on his door: "The Crow's Nest". Bryan accepted his nickname in good part.

One evening just before Easter 1979 Bryan popped his head into the medical cubicle of the Crypt with the casual request, "Just have a look at me feet will you?" The nurse on duty was horrified to see severe swelling and, knowing Bryan's medical history, suspected that his condition had flared up again. She consulted the doctor and it was agreed that Bryan should be referred to hospital immediately. But Bryan would have none of it and grew angry at the pressure put on him to seek further medical treatment. All through Easter he carried out his normal duties but as soon as it was over he agreed to go to hospital. He had made himself almost indispensible and had not been prepared to desert the church at a time when extra services increased the workload of all the staff.

Bryan was admitted to Cookridge Hospital, Leeds and from there he went to Wheatfields, a hospice for the terminally ill. At first he talked constantly of what he would do when he got better — he could not bear to consider the possibility of being parted from the church which he loved and which had been his home for so many years. Finally he accepted the inevitable conclusion of his illness and the real peace he now radiated was a great joy to all his friends. His visitors came away uplifted — and what visitors he had! "You're the sixteenth today!" he would announce with pleasure as yet another figure appeared in his doorway.

His Bible was always in a prominent position and he

talked openly about his faith. "I'm not afraid," he declared, "I'm really ready to go to my Lord."

Bryan died in Wheatfields Hospice on 21st November 1979.

CHAPTER 2

THEIR FATHER'S HOUSE

The year that Bryan left home to join the Army was the same year St. George's Crypt opened. It was the Revd. Don Robins[2] who, as a newly-appointed young vicar in 1930, challenged his congregation to show the love of Christ in a practical way.

"St. George's," he said, "must be a church wherein may be found the life of a Christian family, not as a theory but as a living fact. The tasks that confront us are enormous but the strength of those who trust in God is unlimited. I pledge myself that as far as in me lies, where the battle is hottest and the work is hardest, there you will always find me. To you all I look for eager, adventurous co-operation, deep fellowship and willing sacrifice. Should I look for less, when the cause is so great and it is God who calls?"

The country was in the depths of industrial depression and Leeds, with its dependence on clothing manufacture and engineering, was hard hit by unemployment. The strain of seeking job after job to meet with

2 Don Robins' life and ministry has been recorded in a biography by Paul Glidden, "But who was Don Robins?" publ. James Clarke & Co. Ltd.

the same negative response, could soon undermine a man's self-respect and the anxiety of those with wives and children often came close to despair.

Don Robins saw these signs in the faces of men in almost every street and could not but be moved to action when confronted with such hardship on his very doorstep. If only the men had somewhere to go, somewhere they could get a free hot drink, somewhere they could meet people who cared and would do what they could to help . . . Don decided to open a rest room where men could find such relief and with this in mind he led an inspection of the crypt beneath his church, which had not been used for burials since 1855.

A gruesome sight confronted him — collapsed vaults, exposed coffins, gaping holes in the walls, a crumbling brick roof and a floor of what appeared to be earth, so deep was the layer of dust and debris which covered it. There was no heating, no lighting, no ventilation. It was about the last place anyone would think of as a shelter to welcome the distressed. Anyone, that is, except Don Robins.

His initial foray into the crypt was followed by a sustained onslaught. A hardy band of volunteers attacked the rubbish and grime, and the gaping vaults were covered with canvas. With the installation of an electric light and three oil fires the crypt took on a new look. Members of the congregation provided milk, sugar and cocoa, plus paraffin for the stoves, and with these basic provisions the Crypt Rest Room began to open for two hours each morning. The Diocesan authorities, hearing of these unusual activities wrote to the vicar asking "Have you a Faculty for making such changes to a church?" Don's reply was typically forthright: "Have you a Faculty for keeping it as a dust heap?" The authorities did not bother him again.

Meanwhile the unemployment problem was being aggravated by the influx of men from the north-east and the Scottish borders, who had taken to the road in the vain hope of finding jobs further south. All these men arrived in Leeds with no money and nowhere to stay: many were suffering from illness and exhaustion as a result of sleeping rough, and winter was on the way.

Don determined that as many men as possible would be given the opportunity to spend their nights in the Crypt. This would mean carrying out considerable renovation work as there were no sanitary arrangements and the state of the vaults was beginning to cause concern. So he and his helpers rolled up their sleeves once more, now joined by one or two unemployed men who had benefited from the existing facilities. Matchboarding was used to seal off the vaults and other necessary alterations were made so that on 31st December 1930 the Crypt was able to open as a night shelter. A kitchen staffed by unemployed men provided a simple supper and a breakfast of bread and jam. Papers to read, games to play and various weekly entertainments were provided — to help alleviate the boredom which could be so destructive to morale.

Up to 50 men were accommodated in the Crypt nightly. No beds or bedding were provided, but they did receive warmth, cover, food and, above all, friendship. Soon the number of voluntary staff grew to more than 30, working at varying times of the day and evening. Anyone who expressed the slightest willingness to help was quickly conscripted into service, and all were known to Don by their Christian names, helping to foster a family spirit among the workers. This is still very much in evidence today.

Knowledge of the work going on in the Crypt soon spread and gifts of money, clothing, bedding and food began to flow in. A BBC radio appeal became an annual event and many of those early subscribers have continued to support the work ever since.

The Crypt's voluntary helpers could find themselves engaged in any task from serving cocoa or issuing clothing to typing acknowledgements for gifts received. Eventually some full-time staff had to be appointed; initially these were a night watchman, someone in charge of the office, and a tailor (to mend the gifts of clothing). Today there are more full-time and paid workers, but the Crypt still depends very much on its large band of voluntary workers in all fields of activity.

Don had begun with the men but he realised that their wives and children were equally in need. Soon between 15 and 25 families a week were being supplied with clothing and a Women's Rest Room was opened at a nearby Mission Hall, where unemployed women and the wives of unemployed men could come with their children to receive food each morning.

At Christmas parcels of groceries were distributed and an annual Christmas Tree Service was started to

The opening of the Crypt, 1930. (Don Robin is 4th from the left)

"The Crypt Rest Room, 1930"

which the congregation brought gifts of toys. These, together with others sent in from churches, schools and homes in many parts of the country, were displayed in a Free Toy Shop, where mothers of needy families could choose personal gifts for their children. Up to 100 decorated Christmas trees were delivered to needy homes all over Leeds. Activities similar to these are still going on each Christmas.

The needs and problems of those who came to the Crypt were many and varied. One early appeal leaflet listed some examples of assistance given.

> *"We have helped with rent, railway fares, transport to and from hospital, surgical appliances, spectacles and funeral expenses. We have provided wedding rings and fees, holidays, fuel, invalid foods, furniture, invalid chairs, beds and bedding. We have sheltered stranded families, found lost sons, restored runaway boys to their homes and helped those who have made tragic mistakes to begin life afresh.*
> *We are thankful that in every crisis of life men and women feel that they can come to the Crypt as into their Father's House."*

Don Robins' energy and enthusiasm appeared inexhaustible. As well as the ever-expanding work of the Crypt, his responsibilities included not only the church and parish of St. George's, but also for many years two other Leeds parishes. He was an avowed pacifist, yet active in work among servicemen. He was also Chaplain to the Yorkshire Evening News P.O.W. Club. Whatever came under his charge received his wholehearted involvement — he never directed play from the side-lines but, as he had promised in that first sermon, he was always in the thick of the fray.

From time to time he was troubled with a leg injury which he had received in his school days and was often advised to rest. The very word was anathema to him and one doctor, finding his advice and treatment constantly ignored, refused to accept Don as a patient any longer.

Towards the end of 1947 Don had been showing signs of increasing strain, but his reply to anyone who expressed concern for his health was always, "While God has work for me to do, He will give me the strength to do it." In January 1948 however, he was finally forced to take his doctor's advice and retire to bed. A thrombosis formed as a result of the varicose ulcer in his leg and on the morning of February 3rd he suddenly became very ill and realised he was dying. He called his wife, Alva, and expressed his love for her and his two sons. His last words were for his wider family at St. George's: "Give them all my love and tell them that I love them all very much."

His death, at the age of 48, came as a great shock to the many people who had numbered him among their friends and to the thousands who had supported or been helped by his ministry. It was said, "The light has gone out of Leeds".

Don Robins the man had gone, but the Spirit of God which had filled him and inspired all his work lived on. Under His guidance the work of the Crypt went forward into a new era.

CHAPTER 3

A NEW ERA

After the Second World War the Crypt began to draw not only the unemployed but also the unemployable, the inadequate and the homeless. Their numbers did not decrease as the country moved towards relative prosperity nor, as some had hoped, with the introduction of the modern Welfare State in 1948.

These men had nothing in common with the fanciful notion, still occasionally found today, that the tramp is one who freely roams the countryside unfettered by the pressures and demands of society. The men who came to the Crypt were certainly not homeless vagrants by choice. They blamed their condition on a variety of causes — deprived childhood, wartime traumas, government policies — as well as their own failings.

If the Crypt were to continue to care for all who came a full-time warden was now essential. This post was first filled by a Church Army Captain and then by curates or men preparing for ordination, but the first long-term Warden was Richard Allen.

On the face of it Richard de Courcey Allen was a most unlikely candidate for Warden of the Crypt. His aristocratic name, privileged background and public school education (followed by Oxford and Cambridge) might have created a vast gulf between himself and the men. But the Spirit of God is a great leveller and these superficial barriers were soon shown to be of no importance.

When he came to Leeds in 1953 Richard Allen was no stranger to the ways of the homeless, the wanderer and the alcoholic. As a student he had spent his vacations not visiting his family or friends but staying in the reception centres and hostels — getting alongside the men who used them and living as they did, in order to appreciate their attitudes and understand their needs more fully.

At the Crypt he hoped to continue this approach, in a modified form, by living in a caravan on the church terrace. Having been persuaded that this was not altogether suitable he decided that if he must live in a house then men from the Crypt must share it with him. So a small house in Lofthouse Terrace became Faith Lodge and new possibilities were opened up in the work of the Crypt.

Here was a place where men could live in a proper home, contributing to their upkeep in practical ways as well as by a token charge, and where they could receive sustained help and encouragement as they sought to get on top of their situation and progress to a settled way of life and independence. The stable home background, better living conditions and especially the closer personal relationships which it offered all helped to make Faith Lodge an important step along the road from living outside the community to living within it.

Richard Allen's tremendous optimism made him at first somewhat gullible, and one or two men began to think that here was a heaven-sent soft touch! But he soon learned that hoping for the best in a man does not always mean believing the best of him. He had to accept that some men were natural and compulsive liars and that he should not accept their stories at face value. Whenever it turned out that such a man was actually telling the truth, his exultation knew no bounds!

In Faith Lodge Richard made himself available at all times and often sat up late into the night trying to help a man find a way through some particularly oppressive worry or problem. His diary frequently records fatigue and on 2nd October 1954 he wrote: "Nearly killed myself by falling asleep at the wheel. Car left the road and went onto grass verge. This woke me just in time to brake hard so as not to hit a car in front. . . . Later stopped to sleep for a bit. Arrived an hour late."

In 1959 he married Molly, a doctor, and Faith Lodge moved with him into a larger house in Wellclose Place. Here he and his wife occupied a ground floor flat, while six members of his Crypt family had a bedroom each, with a shared sitting room, kitchen and bathroom.

For two years Don Paterson, a psychology student, shared in the work as a steward combining his duties with psychology research which he hoped would shed light on this little-known section of the population.

Don went on to become Warden of the Crypt from 1962 to 1968.

Richard Allen was particularly moved by the plight of alcoholics and founded the Leeds Advisory Council on Alcoholism, which led to the formation of a National Council. One man in particular posed a challenge which taxed all Richard's faith and ingenuity.

Dave lived at Faith Lodge on and off for many years. He longed to be free of his addiction but was afraid of receiving treatment in an Alcoholic Unit. Several times he agreed to admission but at the last moment his courage failed him and he found some reason for backing out. So month after month, year after year, the struggle went on. What made Dave a special challenge was the fact that he was a Christian and wanted above all else to be a missionary. No decisive victory has yet been won in this long-drawn-out battle. Dave was last seen only two years ago, when he described himself as "a Christian alcoholic tramp". He was still praying regularly and eager to serve the Lord but still in the grip of his addiction.

Most of the men who have lived at Faith Lodge have either been alcoholics or spent time in mental hospital or prison. How does God reveal Himself to men like these? Don Paterson recalls at least one occasion when God used the "foolish" to confound the "wise"[3]. He had been attending a university seminar where various clergymen, professors and theologians

3 see I Corinthians 1:20

had been expounding a passage of scripture in which the symbol of fire was a central theme. Returning to Faith Lodge he was not overjoyed to find that the same passage was scheduled for family prayers. But one of the men present was an ex-fireman. Simply, vividly and with authority he was able to shed more light on the passage than any of the scholars had done! God spoke to this man through the subject he knew most about.

Arthur is another man to whom God revealed a spiritual truth through his own life and experiences. A thief for most of his life, after coming to the Crypt Arthur made an effort to go straight. He went to live in Faith Lodge but was not able to maintain his initial resolve for very long. One day he came to the steward. "There's something I've got to tell you," he said. "Your camera's disappeared — I stole it . . . and pawned it." In shame he held out the pawn ticket. To his amazement the steward forgave him for what he had done and, moreover, went out and redeemed the camera with his own money. "I've been coming to family prayers night and morning for months," exclaimed Arthur, "but I never realised until now what that word 'redemption' really means." After many ups and downs Arthur went on to become a striking witness to the presence and peace of Christ in his life.

When Richard and Molly left Faith Lodge in 1962 their places were filled by Don Paterson and his wife, Pam, who remained until 1968. It was then decided to appoint separate wardens for the Crypt and Faith

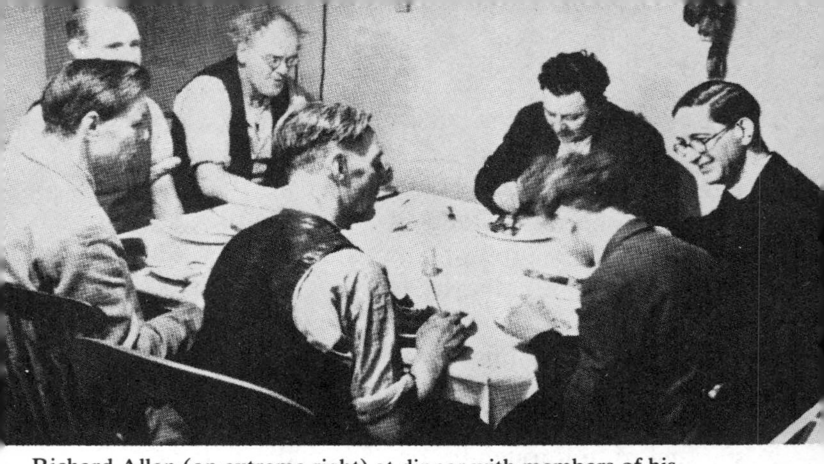

Richard Allen (on extreme right) at dinner with members of his Crypt Family

Faith Lodge, Wellclose Plac

The present Faith Lodge

Lodge so that both areas of the work could receive fuller attention. Don and Pam Blackmore now took over at Faith Lodge and were able to expand the work when the house next door became vacant and was sold to the Crypt. In 1976 the building was put under a compulsory purchase order and the present Faith Lodge was bought and equipped by a local benefactor.

Richard Allen's ties with the work were by no means broken. In 1970 he returned as Warden of the Crypt but within a month he was killed when his car crashed on the M1. He had fallen asleep at the wheel.

Among those notified of the accident was Don Paterson and that night he had a vivid dream. Richard was standing beside his bed, shaking him awake. "Don," he called urgently, "do you know what time it is?" Don told him. Richard was fiddling with his wristwatch. "My watch has stopped," he said, "we 3, must rely on yours now." Then he was gone.

Don knew that such a dream had natural explanations but even so he cannot be sure that it had no influence on his decision to return to the Crypt in 1975 when he was invited once again to become Warden.

CHAPTER 4

DAY BY DAY

Don Paterson is not only an ordained minister but also has a psychology degree and experience of psychiatric nursing. His work at the Crypt makes use of both aspects of his training.

Nearly all the men who come have, in the language of psychiatry, "inadequate personalities". They are simply unable to cope with the demands of society. Many are illiterate, some mentally backward. Some are epileptics, others have personality disorders which make it very difficult for them to make and maintain relationships. Mental illness is a problem frequently encountered, especially in the form of anxiety states, depression and schizophrenia.

There is no substitute for experience when seeking to unravel the causes and effects which have brought a man to the Crypt. The problem he first admits may bear little or no relation to his real needs. Thus a man may come with a request for a food parcel, but tactful probing and a degree of intuition reveal that this is merely an excuse for making contact. His real problem may be that his electricity has been cut off or his wife/girlfriend has left him, or perhaps he is depressed and is seeking a friendly ear and the support of someone who cares.

Whatever the problem, the staff of the Crypt will offer some advice or help. In cases of genuine need a food parcel can be given. This contains a small can of baked beans, a small tin of meat, some tea bags, evaporated milk and bread. This is calculated to keep a man going for a day or two, but not to provide so much that he becomes entirely dependent.

Another way in which the Crypt offers practical help is by providing clothes. There is a large clothing store for men and another for women and children. Each week collecting and sorting clothing takes many hours and items are issued to men on three afternoons and one evening. This is regarded as a very important part of the work for a man must be clean and tidily dressed if he is to find either a job or accommodation. Careful records are kept of what each man receives and if he is requesting a new overcoat or shoes he must hand in the old ones to prove that he is not just after something of value to trade for cash or drink.

The men who come can be just as fashion-conscious and just as fixed in their likes and dislikes as anyone else, and the staff try to suit each man's personal taste. To feel smart and well dressed is something which gives everyone more confidence and self-respect and so clothing issues are regarded as great opportunities for repairing frayed egos.

The daily routine of the Crypt is unchanging, yet every day is different because the needs and problems, and the men themselves, are largely unpredictable.

Each morning the doors are opened at 5.00 a.m. when men who have spent the night elsewhere may come in to have breakfast with those who have slept in the Crypt. Breakfast consists of bread and cocoa. The men must leave by 7.00 a.m. and the night staff then wash up the mugs and tidy the kitchen before going home to bed at about 8.00 a.m.

The day staff arrive at 9.00 a.m. and share a time of prayer together before the Crypt opens again at 9.20 a.m. Men may then make use of the day room and consult Don or one of the assistant wardens about any difficulties. Don normally spends his mornings interviewing — advising on problems with applications for corporation housing or other accommodation, social security payments, debts, legal troubles, hospital appointments and a whole range of matrimonial and personal problems. "Every problem," he says, "involves personal inadequacy and spiritual need." The object is always to advise and encourage a man but also to help him stand on his own feet as far as possible.

During the morning the Crypt must be tidied, swept and disinfected, lunch must be prepared and soup tickets made out ready for the evening. The five assistant wardens to whom these task fall are normally graduates who have come straight from university to spend one or two years at the Crypt. When faced with the routine chores they are encouraged to remember that such things are esential to the men's physical well-being and their human dignity. Even when a man has reached his lowest ebb, if others treat him as someone of value he can begin to believe in his own worth again.

In addition to the issue of clothing, afternoons are taken up with more interviews, correspondence, hospital and prison visiting, various meetings and preparing the Crypt to receive the hundred or so men who come each evening for food and shelter. The evening is the busiest time and a group of half-a-dozen volunteers (a different team each night) arrives at 7.15 p.m. to share in the work of giving out soup. serving in the shop and the inevitable washing-up, but most importantly talking to the men. Some men prefer to sit silently watching television, but many welcome the chance to talk to somebody new.

The Crypt shop has a steady flow of customers buying tea, biscuits, crisps and other snacks. Items like matches, soap, toothpaste and razors are also sold, all at cost price.

A nurse and, on three nights a week, a doctor are available to deal with medical problems and Don is again in his office to receive any newcomer to the Crypt and to review the situation of men already established.

At 9.00 p.m. there is a short service in the Crypt Chapel, led by the voluntary helpers. All the men are invited, though not pressed, to attend. The service is followed by a time of prayer for staff and helpers, while the men settle down for the night. Then Don hands over to the night watchman, who is responsible for the Crypt and its occupants until the following morning.

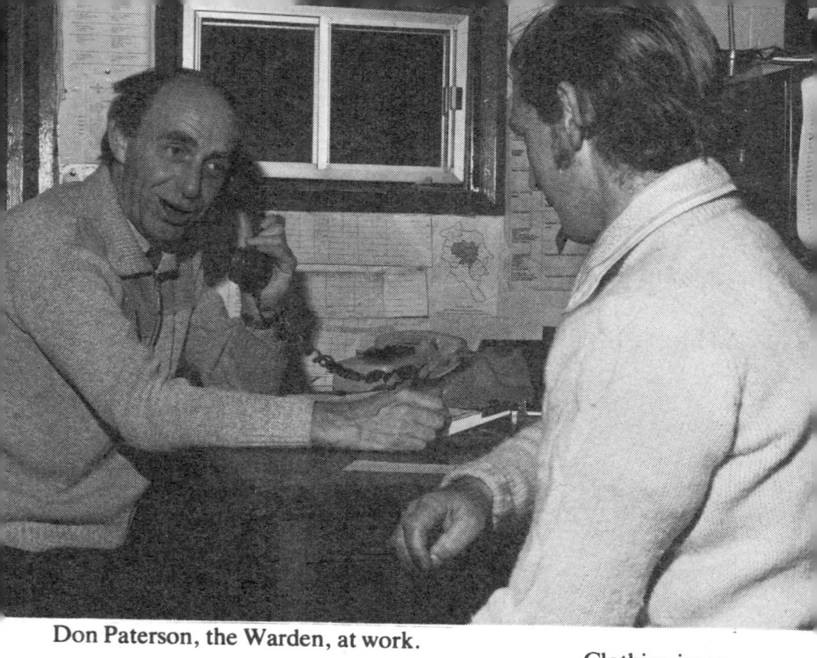
Don Paterson, the Warden, at work.

Clothing issue

Coming out of the Crypt at 10.00 or 10.30 at night is like leaving one world and entering another. Young couples linger in doorways, laughing groups make their way home from the pub, cinema or theatre. The city is full of lights and activity. Yet immediately behind you, world-weary men are sleeping on benches or the floor in what was formerly a place of burial. They seem like a race apart, but are they?

CHAPTER 5

THE STATE TAKES CARE OF ALL THAT . . . DOESN'T IT?

Many of the men who seek help at the Crypt come under the Home Office definition of "persons who have shown a continuing failure to cope with the demands of society, to form personal ties, to find or hold employment, to find a place to live and to respond to rehabilitation or deterrence".4 The Supplementary Benefits Commission writes: "In essence they are homeless people who require preparation for, and help with, independent living, as a result of social disadvantage, ill health or prolonged institutional care or custody".4

Government policy towards these men is illustrated by the 22 Reception Centres administered by the Department of Health and Social Security. These provide temporary board and lodging in the form of cubicled or dormitory bed space, and three cooked meals daily. Medical care and leisure activities (T.V., billiards, table tennis etc.) are available and at a few

4 "Annual Report 1976 of the Supplementary Benefits Commission" Publ. HMSO

centres there is spiritual guidance. If a man has funds he will be expected to pay but if he has no income he will be given pocket money. All the men are expected to help in the day to day chores of the centre.

The aim of the centres is to influence men towards a more settled way of life and each man is given personal attention: his problems are discussed and help or advice offered. The available alternatives to his present lifestyle are put to him and he is helped in his choice. He is allowed to stay until fresh arrangements have been made and generally this period will be one of months rather than days.

Leeds has a new purpose-built centre standing in its own grounds which can accommodate 96 men, but it is rarely more than half-full. The Crypt, on the other hand, nightly receives upwards of a hundred men. Why?

The main reason that men will not use a Reception Centre is their desire to preserve their independence. They know that on admission they will have to sign a statement, to strip and bath, and allow their clothing to be searched. These regulations are essential to prevent misuse of the facilities and to protect the men from infection and infestation. Some men, however, feel that the resemblance between these procedures and those for hospital admission or being taken into police custody is too close for comfort. They may be wary of the "personal attention" they receive, which is in the form of an interview which they are afraid will simply show up their inadequacy.

Other men do not use the Centres because they refuse to accept the standards of discipline and hygiene which are necessarily imposed. One of the Crypt's most colourful characters, known as "Barnsley Bob", did stay occasionally at Reception Centres. He had his own way of demonstrating the extent to which he accepted their standards: as soon as he left in the morning he would head straight for the nearest muddy puddle and commence an exaggerated washing of hands and face!

Reception Centres are just one of the many provisions made by the State for individuals and families who are without accommodation or in financial distress. A man of "no fixed abode" may obtain a daily subsistence payment. Supplementary Benefit, assessed according to need, will provide a man or family with housekeeping money plus rent upon confirmation of the address given. Assistance is also available towards the cost of rates, fuel and electricity, as well as in the form of free school meals, free milk for under-fives and free dental treatment, glasses and prescriptions. Everyone who pays National Insurance contributions is entitled to claim unemployment, sickness and invalidity benefit.

But benefits cannot end poverty. Supplementary Benefit levels are based upon an assessment of the needs of a hypothetical "average" man or family with "normal" needs — debts or the payment of fines cannot normally be taken into consideration and it is assumed that the recipient will spend the money sensibly.

Some men and women are governed by their every whim and impulse and are not able to manage their money without strict supervision. Again, if a man works so sporadically that his National Insurance card has insufficient stamps, or if he is unemployed through his own fault, or if he fails to sign on, he will not be eligible to receive those benefits which depend upon his N.I. contributions. Legislation can never be flexible enough to cater for the vagaries of every individual.

The Welfare State cannot be expected to solve every problem and satisfy every need. Social workers have a professional role to fill but they do not have the resources on their own to make up for all the factors which create disturbed and inadequate personalities and destroy family and community life. They cannot, unaided, break into the "cycle of deprivation" which perpetuates the problems from one generation to the next. Increasingly they are looking to voluntary agencies, including the Church, to help them.

Whatever the State may or may not do, the Christian Church has a responsibility to those in need. We cannot, and should not, expect the State to "take care of all that".

Anton Wallich-Clifford, a one-time Crypt worker, and a founder of the Simon Community[5], highlights this in his book "No Fixed Abode".

5 A pioneering venture begun in London to provide shelter for the homeless and destitute on their own terms. "No Fixed Abode" (publ. Macmillian Ltd.) tells the story of the early days of the Simon Community.

> *"The biggest danger in our Welfare State is that it makes it too easy for all of us to slip out of personal care and concern . . . we should not become accustomed to practising our charity by proxy."*

He goes on:

> *"The consistently homeless . . . are an indictment of all of us who — through ignorance, lack of interest or failure to be concerned — permit a Welfare State to be structured around us like a soft cocoon, cutting us off from the crying needs of our fellow men."*

Another unfortunate side-effect of our Welfare system is the tendency of many who are self-supporting to regard those who receive benefits as idle scroungers and "good for nothings". "If you want to do good, why not help someone deserving instead of wasting your time on a lot of layabouts?" is the sort of comment often made to workers at the Crypt.

It is true that some of those who seek help at the Crypt are undeserving in every social sense of the word: they may be penniless because they have spent their wages (or benefit) on gambling or drink. They may be jobless because they are untrustworthy or because they get restless and move on after only a few days in any job. This kind of behaviour is generally a symptom, of some deep underlying problem which may be of physical, emotional or psychiatric origin. The motto of the Crypt is "For those in Need" — reflecting the belief that God's love is offered in relation to the needs of a man and not to what he deserves. Those needs are both material and spiritual, and the two cannot be separated.

The Crypt is not there to duplicate or undermine the work of those employed by the state. The relationship between the Crypt and government bodies is mutually beneficial and its staff are recognised as providing support for those who reject, do not fit into or fall foul of the State system.

Crypt workers are not there to act as social workers, legal advisers, probation officers, doctors, psychologists or preachers (although all these have been numbered in their ranks). They are there as the Church in action, enabling God's love to be shown to those in any kind of need. The food, shelter and clothing they provide, the practical advice and the sharing of the Gospel all say one thing: God cares.

CHAPTER 6

DUST TO DUST

Until 1962 the Crypt consisted of one rest-room with a small kitchen at the end, a single toilet outside under the church steps, a cramped clothing store and an "office" in a passage. Only about a quarter of the Crypt was in use for the work, the greater part of the building, screened off behind the white-washed matchboarding, was still occupied by the tombs for which it had originally been intended.

The rest-room could accommodate only a fraction of those in need of shelter and large numbers had to be turned away every night because the Crypt was full. This deeply grieved the staff and it was finally decided that the removal of the tombs and their contents should be undertaken so that the whole area of the Crypt would be available for use.

Before this could be done a special dispensation had to be granted by the Home Secretary. This took two years to obtain and during this time all the legacies received by the Crypt were carefully managed so that sufficient capital would be available to set the work in progress.

It was a mammoth operation. There were 700 stone vaults although only about 300 had actually been used for burials. Throughout the work, which took seven years to complete, the Crypt remained open to the men. The Public Health Inspector advised on the measures necessary to ensure decency and privacy and the section being excavated at any one time was sealed off from the rest of the building.

The smell, unfortunately, could not be sealed off: it permeated everything. All who experienced it agreed that it was "indescribable"! At one time it was rumoured that the workmen removing the tombs were about to demand more money and were prepared to strike. But confrontation was averted by one of the men from Faith Lodge, an alcoholic, who had volunteered to work alongside the builders. Sometimes the job made him literally sick but he kept on working. His example encouraged the workmen not to complain and the question of a pay-rise was dropped. The building firm later gave the man a job.

Some members of the church who saw the opening of the tombs found it less gruesome than they expected. One of them said: "If you pulled one end of a coffin it would come open and you would see the pillow with the skull on top of it. If you just tapped the side it all went to dust. It brought home very vividly that the physical body goes."

There were some coffins lined with lead or galvanized iron. The contents of these were very well preserved and one corpse was removed in its entirety and leaned up against the wall as large as life! Most of the coffins and their contents did disintegrate on contact with the air, however, and this meant that the contents of all the tombs could be transferred to one large vault and reburied beneath the church under what is now the entrance to the Vicar's office.

When the work was complete the useable area of

the Crypt was vastly increased. New tiled lavatories were built, a large tiled kitchen, a large clothing store together with a bathroom unit, and a new chapel at the centre of the building. New interviewing rooms and offices were also constructed, letting fresh air and sunlight into the Crypt for the first time.

The dust of death had been banished from the Crypt: now all its resources could be concentrated on the living. The two new rest-rooms can accommodate a hundred men or more. No longer do men have to be turned away simply because there is no room.

Removal of the tombs

Before and After: the Crypt Chapel

Before and After:
the General Office

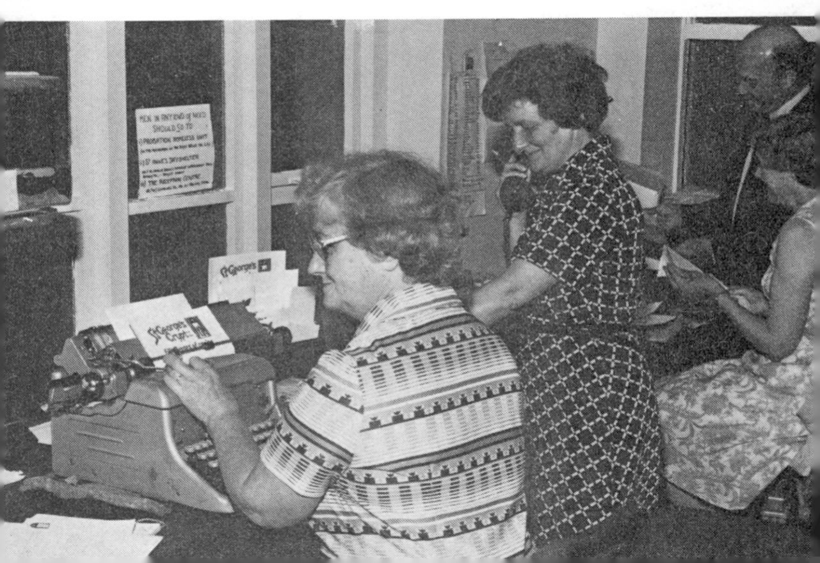

CHAPTER 7

RICH IN FAITH

The Crypt is active in work among women and children, as well as among men. For many years this work was conducted in the Crypt itself but in 1978 a new Family Centre was opened in a portable building in the church grounds.

Ruth Youngman, the Crypt's full-time Family Worker, is able to help families with practical things such as groceries, clothes and bedding, as well as with the assurance that the Lord knows and cares about their needs. She believes that practical help can encourage faith because it shows that the Church cares — and the Church is Christ's representative.

Ruth is in touch with several women from poor families who have gladly accepted the Gospel message and are seeking to grow in the Christian life. Although very apprehensive of going to a church service they enjoy meeting to learn more of God's teaching and to pray together. Each Thursday afternoon half-a-dozen or so women come together for fellowship at the Family Centre.

The informal atmosphere and familiar surroundings help to dispel shyness and some of the women are able to share freely what the Lord has done and is doing for them. Their stories show the truth of St. James' words, "God has chosen poor people to be rich in faith and the Kingdom of Heaven is theirs, for that gift God promised to all those who love Him." (James Chapter 2, verse 6)[6].

Valerie is a wispy-looking woman with a limp. She lives with two grown-up daughters and a son-in-law in a basement flat. Both daughters are mentally-handicapped. From time to time the money runs out and Valerie calls in at the Family Centre in need of groceries.

She was still a young woman when she learned of God's love for her and responded by promising to live her life His way. "My way was such a silly way", she says. "I went dancing nearly every night and spent all my money. I never seemed to have any to spare. When I came to God I started going to meetings at the church most nights. This didn't take all my money like the dancing did so God helped me to use it on sensible things."

Recently Valerie's husband died and she misses him very much. Several of her neighbours and friends are involved in spiritualism and have pressed her to seek contact with her husband "on the other side". Valerie has withstood this temptation. "I know he is in heaven with Jesus," she says simply. "I don't need to ask him what it is like because I know that he is just surrounded with His love. And I know that Jesus will take me to be with Him when my time comes. I don't trust these spirits and voices from the dead. God doesn't tell us to run after all that."

6 Bible references are quoted from the Living Bible version unless otherwise stated.

Valerie can neither read or write but she does know how to pray and can always find something to thank God for:–

> *"Dear Heavenly Father, thank you that you sent Jesus to die for us. He has suffered more than any of us ever have to suffer. Thank you that the Social Security are going to pay my gas bill and thank you for the cooker that the Welfare have got me. Please bless Dot and Dawn and Gordon and cover them with your blood, and my sister Kate who isn't very well and all the people at the Crypt."*

Barbara is a cuddly mum with three beautiful school-aged children. Her house is comfortably furnished and the children well dressed. Barbara is an efficient worker, but underneath it all she is like an insecure and fearful child. She wants to give her children all the things she never had. The bills are piling up, but somehow she manages to keep afloat. She does not draw on the Family Centre for material help so much as for support and encouragement.

She knows that Jesus loves her and has helped her, especially when she has been alone and afraid. "I didn't use to believe in Him but I do now. If you ask Him, Jesus will come into your heart."

The father of her children is a hardened gambler. She has tried to live without him but finds it very hard to be alone. At the moment he is with them, but Barbara is fearful that he will leave again. "If that happens, I'll just have to get on my knees and pray to the Lord," she says.

Miriam lives in the red-light area of town. When Ruth visits her she gives five rings on the doorbell, her personal signal. Miriam likes to know who is there before she will go to the door. Some of her callers are unwanted — former "clients".

She lives a lonely life: a budgerigar and a dog are her only companions. Childhood rejection left deep scars on her personality and the failure of her marriage, with her children being taken into care, only made things worse. She tried both drugs and drink, and sought for love by selling her body.

The flat has peeling wallpaper but new lino (provided by "the Welfare") and the living room is quite homely with religious pictures and texts above the mantlepiece. Beside her chair is a well-worn Bible and a bag containing tracts, texts and prayers. "I'm reading my Bible every day," she asserts. "The psychiatrist was pleased with me and I told him it was the Bible reading that was helping me."

Ruth records a typical visit:

> "After some sharing we have prayer together. Miriam reads a prayer calling on Jesus' victory. Last week she had a drinking bout — the woman opposite is an alcoholic and wants Miriam as a drinking partner, so Miriam needs strength to resist this temptation. The Social Worker is seeing about getting her a move. The dog has had pups and we pray for homes for these.
>
> She went to see her mum last weekend — this was, as usual, a difficult visit. 'They don't really want me,' she says. 'I took her a dress and she didn't even thank me.' We pray about all these things.
>
> Miriam feels relieved and grateful. She will phone if she feels depressed. I invite her to the Thursday meeting but she

hasn't got the confidence to face people yet. But she does know that Jesus loves her and slowly, very slowly, He is healing the scars."

Susan has soft brown eyes, warm and caring. She has had thirteen children, some mentally-handicapped, and they have all had plenty of love. The affectionate nature of the backward ones was sufficient reward to her for the extra attention they demanded. She is now bringing up three grandchildren. Although they are poor she is very generous and never refuses a neighbour who wants to "borrow" money or food, although she knows it may not be repaid.

One Thursday she shared what God had done for her. She had always known God was with her: they had always been poor but God had always provided for their needs. Recently He had saved her marriage. "I know now in a new way that Jesus forgives us," she said. She had become depressed and was tempted to leave her husband. "But God changed him from a hard man into a good, kind man. He says he doesn't believe in God but Jesus must be working in him because he's changed so much."

Then her grown-up son, who had been "sent down" came to believe in Jesus while in prison. Now he had a new motivation for life and had learned to read and write properly. This was another source of joy to her.

Susan and her family live in a four bedroomed, rented house. The walls are damp with creeping patches of black-mould — the result of ancient, leaky water pipes. There are no carpets, just a few threadbare mats on the concrete floor of the living room. Visitors receive an embarrassed apology: handicapped children find it very difficult to achieve bladder control and it seems that no amount of disinfectant can disguise the smell. Bed-wetting children cause the additional problem of rotting bed-linen and mattresses.

Yet Susan's conversation is full of wonder and praise at God's marvellous blessings. She may be poor in material things but is like a millionaire in terms of faith. Her prayers are totally without guile:–

> "Oh God, you are right enough the Gaffer of all of us. Thank you so much for putting Jesus into my heart. If any of the other ladies don't know Him, may He get into their hearts too."

For the first time in very many years, Susan and her family were able to go on holiday in 1980. She sent a postcard to the Family Centre. It read: "Weather perfect and food good, but all that matters is that I know Jesus loves me."

Ruth Youngman (on right) at the Family Centre

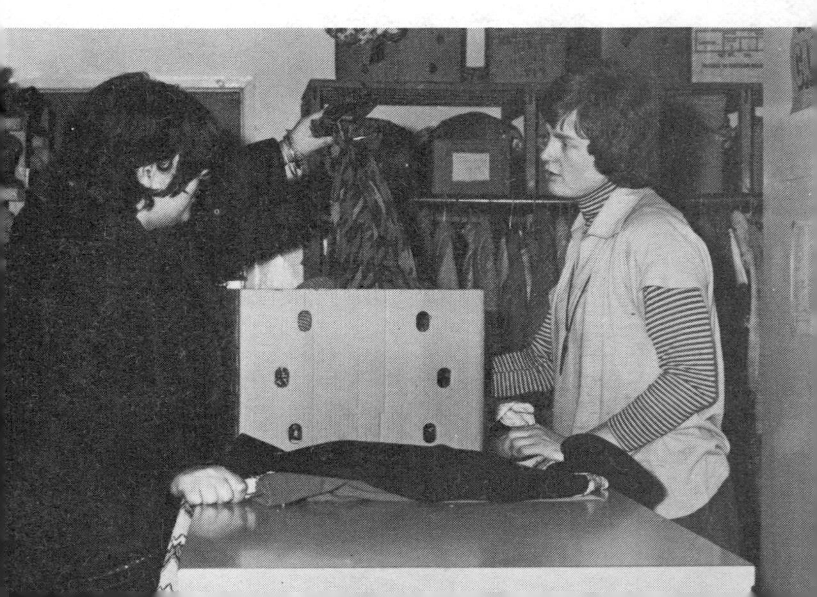

CHAPTER 8

A PLACE TO CALL HOME

For some years it had been felt that a hostel for women and children was needed when, in 1960, the Crypt received a bequest of £1,000 specifically for such a project. This sum was almost half the amount needed to purchase a house in Wellclose Place, just along the road from Faith Lodge. A few years later the house next door was also brought and the two converted into one. When it opened, Crypt House (later renamed Hope House) was the only place in Leeds where homeless mothers and their children could remain together.

Here Ray and Ann Steel are mum and dad to a family of six or seven women and their children (plus their own daughter, Alison). They have had no formal training for this work, although Ann's nursing experience and Ray's trade as a joiner have both proved useful. Their real training has been gained, they say, "in the school of experience".

It was when the family was deep in debt and facing homelessness, while Ray was in a psychiatric hospital, that Ann put her life in God's hands trusting him to bring them through their seemingly hopeless situation. On his discharge from hospital Ray too turned to God and together they began to learn how His power could change things — and lives. Five years passed, during which their faith became deeper and stronger as God dealt with their problems one by one.

Both felt sure that God could use them in some work where the difficulties they had gone through would be turned to some positive value. They were led to Hope House.

Women are referred to Hope House through the courts, the probation office or social services. They are in need of far more than just a place to live: they need a home.

Sandra came from the cells under the Town Hall: her only alternative was a remand centre. Her background is very typical of the women in Hope House. Abandoned by her parents, she grew up in children's homes and went on to approved schools. She felt that nobody cared for her and nobody wanted her. She retaliated against society by stealing, forgery and fraud, and had been in prison four times.

Her search for love led her into two disastrous affairs, resulting in two pregnancies. Both children were placed in care, one in the same children's home where Sandra herself had been. Finally she formed a lesbian relationship. This was often violent, especially when Sandra had been drinking, which she did whenever she had any money.

When she first arrived she seemed thoroughly unpleasant and unlovable. Frequently she wet the bed. Residence at Hope House was a condition of her bail but often she went drinking and stayed out all night. Eventually Ray and Ann had to report her to the police for breaking bail. By this time they were deeply involved with the girl and felt as if they had stabbed her in the back. After three weeks at the remand centre Sandra returned and, although bitter at first, acknowledged that they had done the right thing.

Gradually Sandra formed a strong affection for her new-found "parents" and began to show great interest in the Gospel. She found it difficult to believe that God could forgive her for all the wrong things she had done, because she could not forgive herself. She hated her old way of life, but its grip on her was very strong. After about a year she made a commitment to Christ but the old temptations kept dragging her back. From time to time she tried to return to her former girlfriend, who had now formed a new relationship. Sandra's violent streak was not helped by her anger and jealousy. She committed two further offences and was sentenced to nine months in prison. But at least this time when Sandra is released from jail she will, for the first time in her life, have a home to go to.

Pat was referred through the social services. Her husband was dead and she had been living with another man but they had been evicted from their council house because of massive rent arrears. She had three children, each with a different father. She now suspected that she was pregnant again, but refused to consult a doctor.

One night she awoke with violent abdominal pains — every twenty minutes at first, then every ten. Everyone recognized the symptoms of labour and

Ann called the emergency doctor. He had not yet arrived when Pat felt the urge to "bear down". "Please don't," pleaded Ann as Ray rang for an ambulance. "Hang on!" At the hospital Pat was whisked straight into a delivery room while Ray and Ann waited nervously outside.

When they were called in Pat was sitting up in bed looking very cool and calm. Ann looked round for the baby. "Was it a boy or a girl?" she asked. "And where is it?" "Neither," replied Pat. "I'm not pregnant!"

An eager and anxious audience awaited them at Hope House. Seeing the pans of water put ready on the stove to boil and the torn up sheet which had been prepared in case of an emergency delivery Ann suddenly saw the funny side. In the midst of her exhausted laughter she could barely blurt out the news.

The next day they telephoned the hospital and learned that Pat's condition had been diagnosed as . . . constipation!

But this was not the end of the story. On her discharge from hospital Pat was depressed. One evening she went out and did not come back. When the Social Services could not find her anywhere her children were taken away into care. Eventually Pat was traced in another town, living with another man, but her children remain in care.

It was a phone call to the Samaritans that brought Marge and her children into the Crypt House family. She had married young, largely to get away from home and found that her husband disliked going to work. They soon started a family, but he stayed at home looking after the two children while she went out to earn the money. When she became pregnant for the third time Marge knew that she could not continue to support the family financially but her husband showed no sign of changing his ways. She decided to leave him and went to live with relatives. This was not a happy arrangement and one night, in desperation, Marge phoned the Samaritans. They put her in touch with Hope House.

Those first few days Marge felt that she had hit rock bottom. She felt that everything about her life was a failure — her relationship with her parents, her marriage, even her children — the eldest of whom was handicapped. By the end of the first week, though, she began to feel more at home and started to take an interest in the life of the household.

At that time the Crypt had a Chaplain, Tom Townsend, who visited Hope House every week to lead a Bible study and discussion. This was by no means compulsory but most of the women were happy to attend it. It was a totally new experience for Marge. "Even to think about the Bible was an amazing idea, but actually to read it . . . !" she said.

From the beginning she felt a strange emotion come over her every time Tom spoke of the Gospel. It was not altogether pleasent, yet she was always sad when he stopped and looked forward eagerly to his visits. Something inside her kept saying "I want to be a Christian too" but she did not trust this voice at first and tried to ignore it. She was full of questions about God: "Why?" this and "Why?" that, and especially "Why isn't my little girl normal?"

As time went on the voice became more and more insistent, until she realized that this was something more than her own wishful thinking. Still she held back, for fear of making a commitment which she could not live up to. But she spoke to one or two others about her feelings and started to attend other Christian meetings. She kept promising herself, "When I get a house of my own — then I'll become a Christian."

By now she had been at Hope House for a year or more, waiting for a council house or flat. Eventually she could resist the inner promptings no longer and one evening after Tom had led his usual meeting she went to him and said, "I want to become a Christian." Her own audacity quite amazed her. "I realize now," she says, "that you can't choose the time to do these things. When the time is right they just happen."

Soon the longed-for house became available and Marge and her children moved out of Hope House, but she has not lost her bond with the church and her Christian friends.

Marge knows she can trust God to look after her and the children because He has already brought them through several crises. Best of all she can see His hands upon her eldest child, who attends a Special

Ray and Ann with some of their 'family'

Hope House

School which has a Christian Head Teacher. Here she is making good progress and is already showing particular interest in the Bible.

CHAPTER 9

DOCTOR IN THE HOUSE

"I'm sorry to interrupt the service but the Crypt urgently needs a doctor to help one of the men who is suffering a severe fit. Could anyone help?"

This kind of announcement was becoming a regular feature of Sunday worship at St. George's during the 1960s and early 70s. The men using the Crypt bring with them a wide range of medical problems, many of which are aggravated by their way of life and some the direct result of it.

Since the Crypt first opened, nurses and members of the St. John's Ambulance Brigade had been providing a first-aid service, and in those early days they were called upon mainly to tend painful feet and to administer the occasional dose of aspirin or cough mixture.

In more recent years the nurses were increasingly confronted with serious medical conditions and mental illness — things which required formal diagnosis by a doctor and treatment with specialized drugs, neither of which the Crypt could provide.

In 1973 Leeds had a thriving branch of the Christian Medical Fellowship, several of whose members were regular worshippers at St. George's. One of these was

Dr. Robert Keighley, who was an active member of the church and also a trustee of the Crypt. But it was not until he was tackled by the Warden one day that he realized the depths of the need which lay behind those periodic pleas for help that interrupted Sunday services.

The homeless are entitled to medical treatment under the National Health Service but this requires filling in forms and obtaining certain information which the men often cannot or will not provide. Without these forms the doctor is unable to make his routine claim for payment. The unkempt appearance of some of the men can cause offence to other patients waiting to see the doctor and so they tend to find themselves unwelcome in G.P's surgeries. Hospital casualty departments are no more welcoming as the men are often suspected of simply trying to con a bed for the night.

Once he had been made aware of the need, Dr. Keighley set about finding a way to meet it. What was required was a service similar to that of a G.P., prescribing drugs on the National Health, providing sick notes where appropriate and referring patients by letter to hospital departments when further treatment was necessary.

One by one the obstacles of N.H.S. bureaucracy were overcome and the Department of Health and Social Security gave the proposals their blessing. Eight other volunteer doctors joined Dr. Keighley in setting up a surgery on three nights each week in the Crypt itself.

At its inception, the Crypt medical service was unique. Doctors from many parts of the country have since visited it and similar centres have been set up in other cities, notably Aberdeen, Liverpool and Manchester. For Dr. Keighley, the seal was set upon the service when the Professor of Community Medicine at Leeds University recommended that his students should sit in on one or two surgeries to make sure that they had seen the whole spectrum of medical care operating in this country.

The introduction of a surgery in the Crypt was welcomed both by the local Family Practitioners' Committee and the hospital casualty departments. Far from objecting to the setting up of a rival service, local G.Ps were delighted to be relieved of their obligation towards this section of their patients.

The Crypt doctors were aware of the need to protect this new service from abuse. They soon learned that for every patient grateful for the help he received two were devious and determined to get more than their fair share. Very full record-keeping was essential as they had no knowledge of their patients' previous medical history.

One problem was the peddling of prescriptions and another the danger of some patients saving their drugs until they had accumulated enough to take an overdose. With the co-operation of the nurses and a local chemist, a system was devised whereby patients received only one day's medication at a time. The chemist provides drugs on prescription to the Crypt

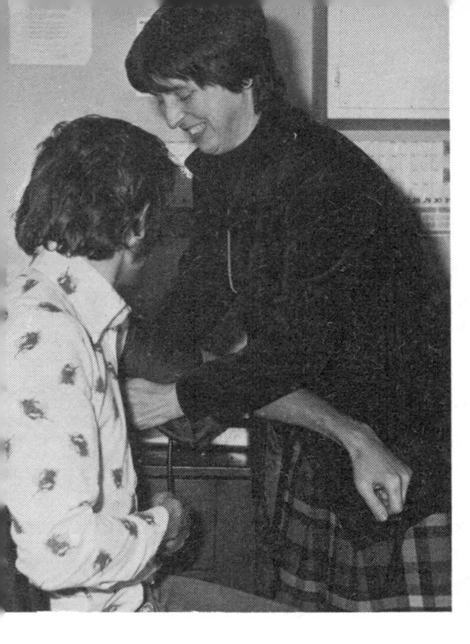

Crypt Medical Service: then and no

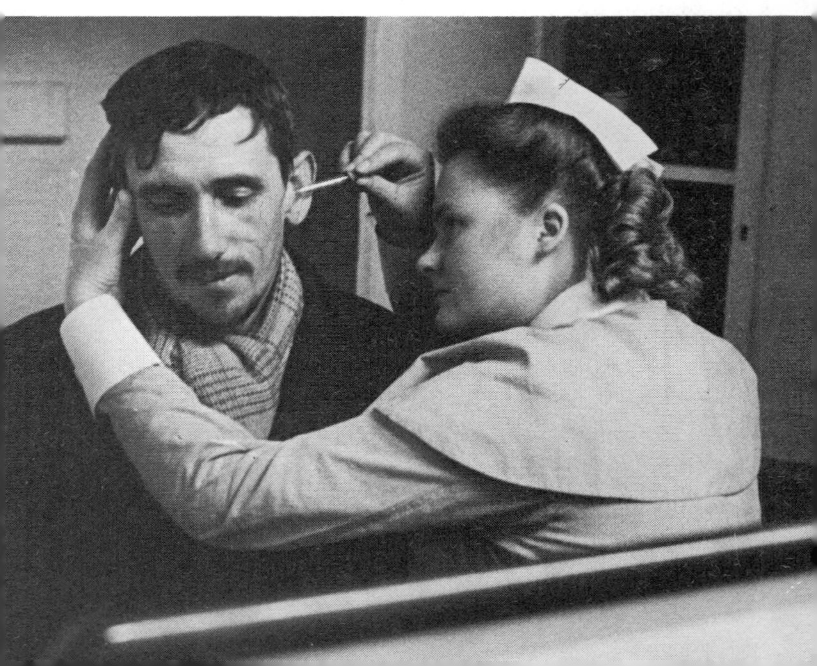

and the nurses have undertaken to keep, issue and record all medications on a daily basis.

The doctor-patient relationship at the Crypt is often a keen battle of wits. Though apparently slow in other respects many of the men quickly get to know the names and relative efficacy of many types of sleeping pill, tranquilliser and other drugs. One addict had been a qualified pharmacist — writing long names on the prescriptions would not delude him! As with any other group of patients, men at the Crypt may be overheard in deep discussion comparing symptoms and treatment.

Many of the Crypt men are unemployable for reasons which cannot be medically treated. They stand next to no chance of finding work and are recognized as unfit. For these men the Crypt doctors will provide a sick certificate for periods of one month, three months or even longer. The men are then able to claim benefit and do not have to make weekly visits to an unemployment benefit office. Great watchfulness is needed to distinguish the genuine from the merely work-shy.

The volume of illness encountered is staggering. For one month in 1975 the doctors analysed the types of medical problems they were treating. Out of 282 patients seen 44 were alcoholics, 35 were bronchitics, 40 had skin sepses and foot troubles. There were 24 schizophrenics, 17 epileptics and 12 severe depressives. In addition patients presented the whole range of ailments normally found in any general practice.

Volunteers who are hospital consultants have proved a great asset as they can "play the old boy network", as one of them put it. This means that they can often obtain an immediate appointment for a patient who is likely to be many miles away by the time a routine appointment is available six or eight weeks into the future. As a result several cures have been achieved in patients who might otherwise have gone untreated.

Amongst the doctors who have been part of the medical team are a neuro-surgeon, a paediatric cardiologist, a geriatrician, a radio-therapist, an E.N.T. surgeon (ear, nose and throat), a psychiatrist, general practitioners and a number of hospital registrars doing a variety of specialist jobs. Thus, three nights a week, Crypt men have direct access to the services of a highly-skilled specialist. Do they appreciate this unusual privilege?

One long-serving member of the team comments, "Many of them are very grateful, but others seem to think that because we work voluntarily we can't be any good. Sometimes I wonder if they think we are just untrained people put in the doctor's room for the evening quite arbitrarily. You know — "Tonight we'll have A working in the shop, B serving soup and C dishing out the pills!" Some men will sit for half an hour receiving expert care and advice from one of the consultant surgeons and at the end of it say 'Thanks very much, but if you don't mind I'd still like to see a proper doctor.'

Asked what was the most frustrating thing about

the work, this doctor replied, "These days people think there is a pill for every ill and the Crypt men are no exception. The worst thing is when you're faced with a patient whom you know no drugs will cure. He's sitting there waiting for you to prescribe a medicine and what he needs is a good job, a stable home and a loving wife. If only we could write a prescription for that."

CHAPTER 10

AN INFINITE CAPACITY FOR BEING LET DOWN

Crypt workers have a two-fold aim: to restore men to a normal way of life in society and to introduce them to the more abundant life which Jesus came to give. Unfortunately, social rehabilitation and spiritual rebirth do not always go hand in hand — a fact which causes many disappointments.

"I seem to be achieving very little here. Very few, if any conversions, though I suppose a few have really availed themselves of the opportunity given them". So wrote Richard Allen towards the end of his first year at Faith Lodge.

Many of the men and women who come to the Crypt see no further than the practical help offered, perceiving little or nothing of the love of God which lies behind all the work. Even so the benefit they derive from the Crypt may be considerable. There is Alec, for instance.

When Alec came to the Crypt he was still in his teens, but already in danger of becoming an alcoholic. Drinking heavily with his friends made him feel big and he often arrived blind drunk. He was no lightweight and the only way to move him was by rolling him down the slope and into the street. The Crypt provided him with the stable influence and encouragement he needed to curb his excessive drinking.

Eventually he met a girl, married and settled down. Some time ago he rang to let the staff know how he was getting on. It was his wife's night out and he was at home babysitting. He is now leading a full family life but has shown no sign of response to the Gospel, although he has heard it many times.

Those men who do respond to Jesus' call to repent, believe and follow have, by no means, seen the last of their problems. It is here that some of the greatest heartaches lie — such as the continuing struggle of Dave, the "Christian alcoholic tramp" and many others who suffer from some form of addiction.

Don Paterson suggests that Crypt workers need "an infinite capacity for being let down". Of course God never lets us down, but things often turn out very differently from what we hope or expect. This was certainly true of Mike.

Mike had been known at the Crypt for nearly ten years, although he only occasionally slept there. One day he arrived in a very anxious state and pleaded with Don to help him overcome his drink problem. It turned out that he had been working for a few weeks, but when he got his wages he had gone out to have a drink. He went on drinking until all the money was gone. The next day he could remember nothing about the night out and had to ask his colleagues what had happened. When they described his behaviour he was terrified in case he should ever get in such a state again. He turned to the Crypt for help.

Don Paterson arranged for him to see the duty doctor and stay at a Christian hostel, providing he could dry out over the weekend. This Mike succeeded in doing and he was safely installed at the hostel where he received Christian care, regular meals and a comfortable bed.

Meanwhile an appointment was made for him to see a specialist for treatment. Mike was finding it almost impossible to stay off drink but the thought of hospital admission and intensive treatment spurred him on. That, he thought, was where his salvation lay. But the hospital did not admit him. Instead it was suggested he return as an out-patient in two month's time. Faced with the prospect of continuing the overwhelming struggle alone Mike took an overdose.

Following this he was admitted to Leeds General Infirmary. There he learned that the nurse in charge of his ward was a former Crypt worker. He saw God's hand in this and turned to Him for forgiveness, committing his life to Him. During the days that followed everything about him bore witness to his new-found peace and joy and to his new purpose for living.

The time came for him to leave the care of the Crypt doctors and register with the G.P. to the hostel. At the Crypt he had received medication for one night at a time but now he had a normal prescription with a covering letter to his new doctor. Just as it seemed Mike's problems were finally under control disaster struck. He received a cash payment of benefit and, with money in his pocket, shared a drink with a friend. The inevitable happened. The alcohol, reacting with his tranquillizers, plunged him into another blackout.

He came to himself three days later many miles away. His mind was deeply troubled but he had only vague recollections of what had happened. Then he read in the paper about the murder of a homeless alcoholic woman. Growing more and more uneasy in his mind, Mike finally went to the police and gave himself up.

Meanwhile Don and the hostel Warden had been trying in vain to trace him. They were particularly concerned at his disappearance because he had paid two weeks' rent in advance (a sign that he had tried hard not to spend all his money on drink in the usual way). They at last found out what had happened from the police.

Mike was charged with murder and at his trial was found guilty and sentenced to life imprisonment. Don Paterson reflected: "As a young Christian of less than two weeks old he had been ensnared by Satan before he had had time to grow in the faith or to appreciate the fullness of the Gospel."

In prison Mike has continued to trust in the Lord. Here at least he is free from the constant temptation to drink. He no longer lives in fear of another blackout. "I was trying to cure myself in my own strength," he confessed, "and I would never have succeeded. Perhaps prison was the only way."

CHAPTER 11

LOAVES AND FISHES

When the Crypt was opened in 1930 its total capital was £3 and its only provisions paraffin for heating and the milk, cocoa and sugar needed to offer the men a nourishing drink. A few weeks later £20 per week was needed to keep open and within two years the weekly budget had risen to £45.

The workers never knew exactly where next week's money was coming from yet come it did, without fail. Don Robins commented: "It was, of course, impossibly foolish — it was as foolish as trying to feed 5,000 people with five loaves and two small fishes. And it had the same result."

From the outset members of the church gave sacrificially and soon gifts of money, clothing, food and other useful items began to pour in from the public. A newsletter/appeal leaflet has been sent to supporters annually since the Crypt opened and within days of its despatch a flood of replies begins, bringing donations large and small. The response is so great that extra volunteers have to be recruited to deal with the mountains of mail.

The Crypt has thousands of subscribers from all walks of life. There are children, students and men and women of all ages, both rich and poor. Churches, schools, business organisations and charitable trusts all play a part.

The home church of one of the assistant wardens mounted an advent project on the Crypt in 1979 which realized over £1,000. An unassuming envelope left on the General Secretary's desk one day was found to contain twenty £5 notes. Smaller amounts are valued just as highly, especially since they often represent real sacrifice. One little boy donated the £10 prize he had won in a competition to grow the tallest sunflower. Some children bring their money boxes and some pensioners give their pension or their Christmas bonus.

Even those who are unable to make any financial contribution can play a valuable part through prayer, and the Crypt Quarterly Prayer Diary is sent to around 1,000 prayer partners. The power of prayer is a sustaining force in every aspect of the work.

The Crypt receives virtually no Government or Local Authority funding, and certainly does not rely upon it. One reason for this is the desire to avoid dependence upon, and accountability to, agencies which cannot fully support the Christian vision. The other is the feeling that Christian work should be financed by Christians, of whatever denomination. Don Paterson sums up this feeling with the words "We are Jesus' people doing Jesus' work with Jesus' resources".

In recent years the Crypt's costs have increased dramatically. This is partly due to the expansion of the work, but also the result of inflation. In 1980 the total running costs of the Crypt, its two hostels and the work among families will be in the region of £65,000.

From the Crypt's earliest days God's power to meet every need, financial and otherwise, has been demonstrated time and time again.

When the Crypt was extended in 1966 a larger boiler was needed for the new kitchen. A new boiler would cost several hundred pounds, and this amount of money was not available, so the staff prayed that God would provide for this particular need. A little later they received a telephone call from an electrical engineer in Harrogate. "You don't know me," he said, "but I've been lumbered with a large gas tea boiler. It's in good working order — it's worth about £300, but I can't get rid of it. I wondered if, by chance, you might be able to use it? You can have it for nothing if you can take it off my hands." When he found out that this was exactly what the Crypt needed the caller offered to pay the expense of installation as well!

The provision of the new Faith Lodge came about in an equally remarkable way. From the autumn of 1975 the staff knew that the house in Wellclose Place was due for demolition. In their search for another building they found an old vicarage which would amply meet their needs. The only difficulty was money — or rather, lack of it! The situation was committed to the Lord with much prayer. By January 1976 a solution was needed urgently so one morning the subject was made the focus of staff prayers. Immediately afterwards, when the office opened, a man arrived enquiring if they had any building projects. He had never visited the Crypt before. Indeed, he had had some difficulty finding it. He could not really explain why he was there now but he had felt a compulsion to come that morning. He only had about 10 minutes spare as he was on his way to the Town Hall. Quickly Stan Raven, the Crypt Secretary, explained the need for a new men's hostel and added that they had seen a suitable property. To cut a long story short the gentleman, who represented a Charitable Trust, agreed to finance both the purchase of the building and the alterations needed to convert it to a hostel.

For the last few years the Crypt's expenditure has been exceeding its income and the difference has been met out of legacies. As costs continue to rise the Crypt is facing a telling test of faith.

"I believe," wrote Don Robins, "that if you see work waiting to be done which God means you to do and dare to take your own pitiably small resources and begin, leaving the rest to God, you will not be failed by Him. This has been our experience all the way through."

CHAPTER 12

SOMETHING MORE — A Personal Postscript

I had seen them, of course, — these "Crypt men" — seen them gathering in the church grounds as supper-time approached, seen them asleep on park benches or wandering through the streets, some in trousers held up with string.

As a Christian I was disturbed that such people exist in our society. Nevertheless, I had sometimes, like the religious men in Jesus' parable[7], crossed to the other side of the road to avoid encountering them. These men frightened me.

Ignorance was, I think, the main basis for my fear. For some reason I imagined that these men were different from others, that they did not share the same basic human needs and feelings as everyone else. Their way of life was so different, their appearance so unorthodox, their attitudes so unfathomable. I felt I had about as much in common with them as I might have with beings from another planet.

7 see Luke 10:30-37

If I am honest there was another reason why these men made me feel uneasy and embarrassed. It was guilt. Each one was a living accusation of MY inactivity, MY apathy, MY negligence in the face of human suffering and need. I knew that Christ would never pass by on the other side.

As a student, I had several friends who helped at the Crypt, but I fought shy of it. I persuaded myself that my sheltered, middle-class upbringing would be resented by the men and that I would almost certainly do more harm than good. I just wasn't cut out for that kind of thing. Occasionally my conscience nagged me — "It's the knowledge of your own inadequacy, the fear of being put on the spot, that's really stopping you," but I refused to listen.

For ten years I continued to worship regularly at St. George's, set in my idea that I had nothing to offer the Crypt and that it looked for nothing from me. A small donation to the annual Crypt Appeal effectively muzzled my conscience. By now I had a husband, a home and two young children to care for — how could I be expected to take on anything else?

Then came the suggestion that I write something in connection with the Crypt's 50th Jubilee. I had always been interested in writing and had already produced a few pieces for the church, so I agreed. "There you are," I told my conscience with a fair degree of self-satisfaction, "This is the way in which God means me to serve the Crypt." But that was only the beginning.

I read any material I could find about Don Robins, about the work, about the sort of men who came. I spent time at the Family Centre and went on a few home visits with Ruth Youngman to learn more about this aspect of the work. I interviewed numerous people who had any connection with the Crypt past or present. Eventually I had to face up to what I had been avoiding for so many years: I could not presume to write anything about the work unless I became involved with it myself.

When I could put off the confrontation no longer I ventured into the Crypt one Friday evening to join the regular band of volunteers, Before I knew it I found myself involved in a discussion between several of the men and two other volunteers on the subject of marriage. As I was the only helper that night who was married, they genuinely wanted to hear my point of view. I did not feel awkward after all.

After that first evening some of the men regularly asked after my two children. I was surprised that they remembered — even more so that they were interested. God had at last succeeded in getting me involved in the work of the Crypt. Strangely, He had smoothed the way for me by means of the very things which I had imagined exempted me from service — my interest in writing, and my family. Surely God has a gentle sense of humour!

I soon realised that the men who come to the Crypt are not so different from everyone else. Their conversation turns around sport, women, politics, money — with a few ribald jokes thrown in — just like any group of men anywhere in the country. There was plenty of back-chat and leg pulling, but through it came the impression that they shared a family feeling — these men cared for one another. (This impression was confirmed when I learned that on the death of the oldest and most cantankerous of their number all the men clubbed together to buy a plant in his memory for the Crypt chapel.)

Many of the men are still young and the most noticeable thing about them is their capacity for self-deception. "Half the blokes who come here are nutters," asserts one man. "I'm not like that. I don't need this place, I've got a flat, I have. I don't need to mix with the likes of them. I don't need to come here at all." Yet here he was nevertheless. Another declared, "I'm not homeless, me. I'm just temporarily between lodgings." He had been "temporarily" at the Crypt for the past three years. But self-deception is a capacity which we all share.

I began to wonder whether the reluctance to become involved which many people feel is the result not of the supposed difference of the Crypt men but, in fact, their sameness. Could it be that we shy away from these men because they force us to acknowledge the aspects of our human nature which we prefer to ignore? Their predicament highlights man's weakness and inadequacy and brings home, with painful clarity, the truth of the words uttered so calmly in many of our churches Sunday by Sunday — "we cannot save ourselves".

When we face up to the practical implications of what was formerly mere head knowledge God leads us into new understanding of His nature and new adventures in Christian living. I would like to share just one of the things which God has begun to teach me about the Christian life as I have worked on this book.

From the outset I was struck by the way the Crypt in those early days was the concern not of a select group of specially gifted people but of the whole congregation of St. George's. It was not a separate project but an integral and natural part of the life of the church.

I realised that this was exactly as it should be. For the Church is something far more than a group of believers meeting to pray and worship God together. It is no less than the Body of Christ and every Christian is a member of that Body. Every Christian, therefore, shares the responsibility for reflecting the love and compassion of Christ. The Bible repeatedly urges us to live up to our calling.

> "Dear brothers, what's the use of saying that you have faith and are Christians if you aren't proving it by helping others? Will *THAT* kind of faith save anyone? If you have a friend who is in need of food and clothing and you say to him, 'Well, goodbye and God bless you; stay warm and eat hearty,' and then don't give him clothes or food, what good does that do?
>
> . . . Faith that doesn't show itself by good works is no faith at all — it is dead and useless."
>
> James 2:14-17

> "Let us stop just *SAYING* we love people, let us *REALLY* love them and *SHOW* it by our *ACTIONS*."
>
> 1 John 3:18

> ". . . as we obey this commandment *TO LOVE ONE ANOTHER*, the darkness in our lives disappears and the new light of life in Christ shines in."
>
> 1 John 2:8

This means that every Christian can, indeed should, be actively involved in helping others, whether in a venture like St. George's Crypt, or some other form of service. No qualifications are needed except the love of Christ. God does not call all Christians to be social workers, pastors, or preachers, but He has commanded us all to LOVE. Love is not a spiritual gift which God bestows upon a chosen few, but is part of the fruit of the Spirit, which should be growing in every Christian heart.

On one occasion, when Don Robins was asked how effective the Crypt was in changing the lives of those who came he replied, "It seems effective enough. But that's not its primary purpose. It does not really exist to change other people's lives, but only as evidence that our lives have been changed."

It is when we are willing for our lives to be changed that the excitement really begins. The story of the Crypt proves that when Christians are actively prepared to live as members of the Body of Christ new revelations of God's wonderful love and power come cascading down. We see that He is infinitely greater than the religious figurehead which we so often make Him.

Our LIVING as Christians will speak far more effectively than any words. One man who came to the Crypt commented, "If you had talked to me about religion I would have argued with you and called it a load of rubbish. But I can't argue with what you're doing. There must be something more to your God than I bargained for."

"Who is like the Lord our God, who is seated on high, who looks far down upon the heavens and the earth? He raises the poor from the dust, and lifts the needy from the ash heap, to make them sit with princes, with the princes of His people."

Psalm 113:5-8 R.S.V.

The God of whom the psalmist wrote has not changed. He still has power over heaven and earth. He still "raises the poor from the dust" — not by extending a finger from on high but by coming down and meeting men and women in the dust itself. In the man Jesus He fully entered into all our human griefs and sufferings: he knew hunger, homelessness, abuse, rejection, pain and death. He made the ultimate sacrifice for the human race He loves so much. In doing so He conquered the power of Satan over us.

Jesus invites us to enter into His victory and inherit the eternal life He has won for us. Accepting His invitation to "Come, follow me," may prove costly, as the rich young ruler discovered.[8] But if we shrink from this commitment, we shall surely miss the greatest adventure that life has to offer.

8 see Mark 10:17-22

Not so very different after all . . .